MARC'S MESSAGE

POETRY BY JOSÉE THERRIEN

COVER ARTWORK BY MARC SABOURIN

Cover artwork by Marc Sabourin

Design: Linda T. Anderson

This book was printed in the United States of America.

To order additional copies of this book, contact:
Xlibris Corporation
1-888-795-4274
www.Xlibris.com
Orders@Xlibris.com
116628

Reality:

The quality or state of being actual or true.

Actual:

Based on fact.

True:

Sincerely felt or expressed.

Feeling alone

is nothing

compared to being alone.

We always think the best things are coming up.

We never really think this is it.

What is a minute is an eternity.

The world doesn't believe in today.

It believes in yesterday

and fears tomorrow.

For the pain and sadness we feel,

hell is real.

Am I drowning in unconsciousness
without being conscious of it?

If nothing ever hides,

then what are we so afraid of inside?

What goes in must come out

in the way

that best expresses the sickness.

The lights are on at home,

but he'd rather be outside in the dark

where there's life.

I can see them so clearly.

Is that really them . . . or is it me?

This moment can't last forever.

It will end somewhere

and it will be forgotten.

The world changes

and if you don't change with it,

you're stuck in the past.

Maybe forever.

We strive to become satisfied
with life's beautiful gifts,
but sometimes we are not fully satisfied
until we escape for a little while.

We eventually come back down to earth
and have to deal with what we have
caused our bodies and find where our
minds have wandered . . . out of this
reality.

Some people know just the right words

to say about happiness

but never apply the actual happiness.

. . . and I was just a body walking.

If I wanted to, I could let the world die,

along with my lie.

It's the madness in this world that would make it all end.

When we're too tired and out of dreams.

Open up your eyes and see that the world is more than just a place, we are more present than we seem.

When I cry, my tears aren't just a sign of sadness, my heart is breaking, my soul shuts down. My feelings are so real. You have no idea, do you? You're not as vulnerable as you should be, your soul is on a free ride.

I want you to see me like I see you. Can't you love me like I love you? When I say I'm sorry, it's from the bottom of my heart. Look deep into my eyes and tell me you don't see me.

Just like the city,

I'm in and out of the darkness.

Hell is for souls that never tried.

Your mind kills you as you betray it.

You leave your body and everything behind,

and you don't know where you are.

I can't see; I can't speak in this world.

I said, "This isn't real," but I didn't believe it.

It's a place that we don't want to see.

There's no mercy in hell.

Lost somewhere in time, we are not here.

But at least with the illusion,

my heart carried me home.

Either fear will take us over
or we will fight through.

We feel bad when we know

the world out there

is moving faster than us.

We feel even worse when we speed up

to catch up.

Don't you know it's rushed?

An addiction;

loud enough to cover the silence.

The world will catch up to me

if I don't let the truth out.

Don't bury it down for it deserves life.

The only control we have

is over ourselves.

We rebel against the world

to prove that we are imperfect,

because everything hides behind

the perfect illusions of this life.

There are no secrets.

The answers lie within.

I realize now that

what I thought was the world's dream

is actually my own.

I want to find in you,

what I find in me,

what there is in all of us.

It's never what we see,

it's what we feel.

My attitude can be questionable
to the world.

But there's a reason for it,
so question me.

Don't let your dreams wake you.

Wake your dreams.

Sometimes we never want
the storm to stop,
because chaos beats reality
when you want it to.

But reality can be clarity,
and clarity soothes the soul.

I have to live like a normal person

in a free spirit's body.

Well, sometimes,

sometimes it's not free.

Look. Stare if you want to.

Just don't close your eyes
and let the world pass you by.

When you feel lonely
or not good enough,
just get through it.

We're not as good as we look,

we're all weak in the same ways.

The dream is at the edge of reality.

Take risks but don't jump off.

There's no way out of it
but through it.

Out of hell, out of fear,
out of the darkness
that lies somewhere underneath it all.

Through hell,
through fear,
through the darkness.

All the beauty in life

comes out at night

when our souls are dreaming

of a better world.

Life is all we know.

Live is all we do.

Even after we die,
there is more life to live.

Life is a mission.

To each their own path to truth.

A moment means more

than forever.

See who's alive

to see if you're alive.

This moment is forever.

I will never die.

It's when you're looking for truth
that you find it more and more.

Break through space and time

to grow.

You can embody what you own

because it is who you are.

This is what life is,

tears and torture

until we figure out it's not so bad.

We're alive and we're free.

We know nothing before

or past the soul.

All we can do is live

to become better human beings.

There's the world beyond
and the world inside.

There is no right rulebook for life,

because what seems wrong to you

might be acceptable to me,

and that's how we learn our lessons.

Habits live unconsciously inside of us.

The only way to break through

is to make nothing a habit.

Could a negative experience

be worth a hundred dollars

just like a positive one could be?

If your dreams are big,

your chances can't be small.

To live young forever,

we must live for yesterday,

today and tomorrow all together.

Things take time

and it's human nature for us

to want things to get here right away.

You have to fall in love with the

moment;

otherwise you're going

to miss out on your life,

all your life.

My life goes by like a story

but more, recently.

I see myself as "she."

And I always think of others.

They're in there too.

So,

what do I have that it takes?

I have heart.

I have too much love

and that's how I fall.

I fall a lot.

But in my story,

I do what I want.

Keep believing.

No one can change your beautiful life.

You create yourself.

The dream, the beauty, it exists.

I assure you from where I am,

high, almost from heaven,

I see you world and nothing ends.

We are the pioneers of today

because we look at yesterday

and understand

what tomorrow will bring.

I will follow my dreams . . .

it's the only way.

The silence is much more special
when you listen to it.

You can hear heaven from here.

Live forever,

right now,

today.

The dream is the only thing we have.

So when you want it,
you can get it.

Just go for it.

The dream is yours.

It's happening,

we're coming together.

Look around . . .

love and inspiration have our hearts.

Can't you see the greatness?

It's been there all along.

We couldn't see it.

Can you feel it?

It's happening before our eyes.

We have changed,

we are fulfilled.

We are the beautiful humans that fill
this life.

With joy.

This day without you

When I close my eyes
I picture you near;
I open my eyes again
and you're not here.

I've learned to shut my eyes
to feel your presence.
Just like in a dream,
I see you so clearly.

I hear you saying I love you,
keep going, don't give up.
I feel you touching my heart.
Our souls are never apart.

You've been gone too long,
but you've changed my life.
Everything reminds me of you.
This day without you.

Author's note

Marc Sabourin, my late father,
was a wonderful human being.
Although his struggles were great,
he dreamed of a beautiful world.

He wanted to see all individuals
being loving, true-to-themselves and
especially considerate of each other's
hearts.

I wish you the best in your beautiful
lives.

Josée Therrien

CPSIA information can be obtained at www.ICGtesting.com
Printed in the USA
LVOW082319130712

290014LV00001B/24/P

9 781477 132951